I Used to be Normal

Dealing with mental health issues as a married father of three. While trying to keep my world together and the struggle between asking for help and being embarassed that I was falling apart.

Mr. Dean E Kresila

ISBN: 1-4565-8003-5
ISBN-13: 9781456580032

Dedication

Dedicated to the memory of my parents

Jean & George Kresila

Table of Contents

Acknowledgments   vii
Introduction   ix

Chapter 1: I Really Was Normal   1

Chapter 2: My World Gets Shattered   5

Chapter 3: Mom's Cause of Death   17

Chapter 4: Things Seemed Normal   21

Chapter 5: Someone to Lean On   25

Chapter 6: Fast-Forward to 2000   29

Chapter 7: What's Happening?   37

Chapter 8: Treatment   43

Chapter 9: Day to Day   47

Chapter 10: How Much Information
    and to Whom?   51

Chapter 11: Time   55

Chapter 12: Money   59

Chapter 13: Regrets   63

Chapter 14: The ABCs of Mental Health   67

Chapter 15: Mind Control   75

Chapter 16: The Internet—
   Helping or Hurting?   77

Chapter 17: Disconnected   79

Chapter 18: Journaling   81

Chapter 19: Man's Best Friend   87

Chapter 20: Superhuman Strength   89

Chapter 21: Final Thoughts   91

Chapter 22: Update   95

Acknowledgments

To my wife, Charisse, without whom this book would not have been written. You believed in me even when I didn't believe in myself. For over thirty years, you've known when to push and when to pull, when to lead and when to follow. And always you have given unending love and support.

To all my family and friends, whether you knew it or not, your love, friendship, and support got me through the hard times and made the good times even better.

Introduction

First, you should know that I am not an author. I have no writing experience and no college degree. I am the last person I would have thought would be writing a book.

But I hope that in writing this book, which by the way I would have found useful, I might share my story with others who are going through what I have been and continue to go through. You see, for more than five years, I have suffered from agoraphobia. I titled this book *I Used to be Normal* because that's just what anyone who knew me would have thought. I was "normal," the guy next door. I was a husband, father, son, and a brother. I was a hard worker, someone who likes sports, cookouts, and all the other things that "normal" guys do and enjoy.

I really believe that there are many aspects of this illness that are unique to men. I am in no way saying that it's harder for men than it is for women. But I do believe that each gender has its own set of unique problems. At the risk of sounding sexist, it's just that if a women, especially a mother, stays home all day, most people wouldn't think twice about it. She is called a homemaker. But if a man stays home and does not work, people would most likely question it. Men are raised to be "the head of the household" and "the breadwinner." So not working and being at home all day, every day, is an instant blow to a man's attitude about himself. It can, and did, lead quickly to depression.

My life seemed out of my control. I felt less and less comfortable in social settings. I was easily startled and angered. I was eventually diagnosed with agoraphobia, obsessive-compulsive disorder, depression, post-traumatic stress disorder, and a few other emotional health problems as well.

For a long time, I believed I could handle my problems by myself. I bought books and searched online to learn all I could. Ultimately, I just got worse and realized that I needed help. One of the problems I had was just admitting that something was going on that I could not fix myself. Another problem that I had, and I believe that others must also have, was my reluctance to reach out to those close to me, and admitting that I was hurting mentally and emotionally. So if you or someone you know are going though something similar, I hope this book will be helpful as you journey on the path to healing.

Chapter 1
I Really Was Normal

I am the youngest of four sons. I was born in 1959, to George and Jean Kresila in Cleveland, Ohio. We lived in a three-bedroom, one-bath home on the far-west side of Cleveland. My parents both worked in factories and made a decent living. We didn't have a lot of money, but we always had enough to live a good life.

For most of my childhood we spent our summers camping. So I grew up outdoors, spending time swimming, playing in the woods, and sitting in front of a campfire for hours each night. The campfire was a place for occasionally deep discussions among kids and adults.

I went to public schools and was an average student. I graduated from high school in North Olmsted, a suburb of Cleveland, in 1977 and worked in a fast-food place in the local mall. It was there that I met my wife, Charisse, and most of the friends I had at the time. I worked from the ages of sixteen to twenty at the restaurant. I had a great life and was very social. We would go out seven nights a week, and I had two or three really great years.

A few months before my twentieth birthday, I really felt like I was at a dead end in terms of employment or career. Some of my friends had gone on to college, and others had gotten good jobs. I had stayed in my fast-food job because it was a fun and easy job. It paid me enough money to hang out with friends and have a good time. But as I got older, I realized that I should think more long term.

It was then that my best friend Pete and I decided to join the army. We were going into the same field, working as heavy-equipment operators. We were told we would stay together for most, if not all ,of our enlistment. After we signed up and made the commitment, we sat down with military job counselors. Based on his test scores, my friend was talked into going into a different field, which made sense for him because after the army he could get a good job that was more suited to him.

When I met with my job counselor, I was told that I would have to wait for up to six months to get into my chosen career. I was extremely impatient and wanted to go into the army right then and not wait for six months. In hindsight, I was afraid that if I didn't go right then, I would change my mind and stay at my fast-food job. So the salesman, I mean counselor (ha ha), gave me three choices: two really crappy jobs and the one that they really wanted me to take, which was in the military police.

Now before that moment I had never even thought of a career in law enforcement. But I was impatient and desperate to get into some type of real career. And the counselors did a very good sales job by telling me how great it was to be a MP. So I signed the paperwork, and within a few days I was on my way to basic training. Walking to the gate at the airport, I knew I had made a huge mistake, but I felt there was no turning back now. So I said my goodbyes and got on the plane.

Chapter 2
My World Gets Shattered

In September 1979, I'd been in the army for just over two months. I was stationed in Anniston, Alabama. I had been pulled from training after I told my commanding officer that I had withheld information on my enlistment papers. I hadn't told them that just two years earlier the army had denied me entrance due to an irregular heartbeat. I had been diagnosed with the condition as a teen and had received treatment for about three years, until it had gone back to a normal heartbeat. But after the rumored death of a guy in another company while doing physical training one morning, I thought it best to come clean. At first, after some medical testing, the army said that it would let me stay in.

But my mother wasn't done yet. She wanted her baby boy home, so she got all my medical records from our family doctor and sent them to my company commander. When the doctors on the base saw my records and put a name to my irregular heartbeat, they decided they didn't want to take any chances. So they started the discharge process. The officers and sergeants kept me around for weeks, because I had been working for them while waiting for all the medical issues to be worked out. I was basically an office assistant, answering phones, typing, and filing. During this time, I saw other guys get discharged for various reasons, but my commanders had gotten used to me working in the office, so I was kept for a while longer.

One afternoon while manning the phones, I answered with the standard "Company B-12th Battalion, may I help you?" To my surprise, it was one of my brothers, which caught me totally off guard. My first thought was that I would get into trouble for receiving a personal call. But my brother quickly told me to come home because my mom was in the hospital. I actually was due to discharge within one or two days. He really didn't give me many details about what was wrong with my mother, only that she had been there for two days. She was unconscious, and the doctors were still trying to diagnose what was wrong with her.

I put my brother on hold and asked my sergeant when I could go home. He said that the paperwork was en route, and it could be as early as the next day. I told my brother this, and we said we would talk the next day. I was concerned, but my brother really hadn't given me the impression that my mom's condition was serious. So I went about my business and looked forward to going home as soon as the next day.

Later that evening, I was upstairs sitting on my bunk. I was by myself because the rest of the company was out on a bivouac (camp-out). The public-address system clicked on, and my company commander's voice told me to report to his office. Generally speaking, recruits didn't talk to company officers. We usually talked only to sergeants. But I had been around all of the commanders while working in the company office, so I felt comfortable around most of them.

In hindsight, I was already in denial about how serious my mom's condition might be. When I went in to see the lieutenant I was surprised that he wanted to talk about my mother. He must have thought that I knew that's why he called me down, because he didn't waste any time. As soon as I walked in, he asked me to sit down. I barely was in the seat when he told me that the Red Cross had just called him and asked that I be sent home immediately. He said they had told him that my mother's condition was grave, and they did not expect her to make it through the night.

To say I was stunned would be a huge understatement. For the first time in my life, I felt a physical response to someone's words. I felt a tightness in my chest, and it was hard to breath. There also was pain in my stomach. Mentally, it was as if I was having an out-of-body experience. I was just numb, and none of this seemed real. I remember tears forming in my eyes, but I was sitting in front of my commanding officer, and I fought like hell to hold back those tears. For a little bit, while my lieutenant was talking, I just kept thinking that this was some big mistake.

Within a few minutes, I had convinced myself that it was indeed some mistake and that my mother was going to be just fine. All I thought about after that was "I'm going home." My lieutenant told me to go pack all my stuff. While I was upstairs, my lieutenant got on the phone to order me a bus ticket, and his wife was at home trying to get me an airline ticket. When I came back down I threw my duffel bag into his truck, and we headed to the bus station.

There was no way that I could have known, nor been prepared for, what was to come over the next thirty or so hours.

Anniston, Alabama, seemed like a small town when I was there in 1979. I really never saw much of it. When I had arrived for basic training, it was about one o'clock in the morning, and we were taken straight to the base, Ft. McClellan. And by the time my lieutenant and I got to the bus station, it was getting dark. When he dropped me off, he asked me if I had any money. I don't recall exactly how much I had, but it wasn't more than a few dollars. So he reached into his wallet and handed me twenty dollars and told me to put it in my sock. Apparently, the station wasn't the greatest area to be alone at night. We said our goodbyes, and he drove off.

I had no sooner gotten my ticket and sat down than the guy behind the counter told me, as I was the only one there, that he was closing up. I would have to wait outside for my bus. The station closed at 9:00 pm., and my bus wasn't due until 12:30 a.m. There wasn't even a bench outside the station, so I threw down my duffel bag and sat for a while. I'd been up since about 4:45 am. and was really tired.

It wasn't long before I was asleep on the ground with my bag as a pillow. I might have slept for a little less than an hour when the bus pulled up. There weren't more than three or four people on it. We were headed to Atlanta, Georgia. It was about a two-hour trip. I was exhausted but unable to sleep. At the Atlanta bus station, I had to take a taxi to the airport. It was a good thing my lieutenant had given me some money, because I would not have been able to pay for the taxi.

At the airport, I had to wait another couple of hours for my flight. So I just sat by myself as time dragged on and on for what seemed like forever. The flight made a stop in Cincinnati, Ohio. But after we landed and people boarded, we could not take off because of fog. So once again I had to sit and wait. It was about thirty or forty minutes before we took off. I had gotten only an hour or two of sleep and eaten just a few things out of vending machines. From the time I had been dropped off at the bus station in Anniston until I arrived in Cleveland, it had been seventeen or eighteen hours. Under the circumstances, being rushed home because my mother was near death, the trip should have been hell. But I had totally convinced myself that there had been some mistake and that she would be fine, sitting up in her hospital bed waiting for me to get home.

When I got off the plane, my brother Dennis and his wife, my brother Jim and his fiance, and Charisse were waiting for me. It was so great to see them. I had never really been away from home, and it had been about ten weeks since I had seen them. The mood was pretty light. They kidded me about my hair (or lack of it) and about my weight (or lack of it, as I had lost about forty pounds). There were no detailed discussions about my mom. I was afraid to ask, and I think they wanted to give me some time to just get used to being home again. But unfortunately it reinforced my thought that mom was going to be alright.

They told me that it would take about an hour to drive to the hospital and rather than wait for my bag, I should just get it later. Mom had been at an amusement park when she got sick so the hospital wasn't near our home. When we got to the hospital, we went to the family waiting room, where I saw my other brother Rick and my dad.

I hugged my dad, and he just broke down crying and walked away. We all talked for a while. I was trying to put off going in to see my mom, after the way my dad had behaved. I started to realize that my mom's condition was worse than I had convinced myself. After a few minutes, I gathered myself and started to go in to she her. My brother Rick quickly stopped me at the door. He tried to prepare me for what I would see when I went in. But I have always been impatient as hell so I barely listened to a word he said. I pushed past him and went in. I took a few steps toward her bed and just froze. Even if I had listened to my brother's every word, I would not have been prepared for seeing my mother like this. I had just spoken to her on the phone a few days before, and she was fine. And I had really talked myself into thinking that everything I had heard over the last twenty-four hours was wrong, and she really would be alright. It is not possible for me to fully describe how it hit me, and how I felt both mentally and physically at that moment. She was unconscious and hooked up to a bunch of machines. The sound of the respirator will be in my head forever. So there I stood, frozen in place, for a few minutes, and when I was able to move again, I just ran over to the window in her room and broke down. I stood there sobbing and staring out the window, praying that this was not real. I stayed about five minutes, but I could not summon the strength to look at her. As I left, I never even looked in the direction of her bed. I walked out without having touched, kissed, or even said a word to her. Out in the family waiting room, everyone came up to talk or hug or whatever, but again I ran to a window in silence. I believe if it had been a door I might have run out and never stopped running.

A little bit later, as I stood looking out the window, I saw my best friend Pete in the parking lot. I could not believe my eyes, because he had gone to basic training a few weeks after I did, and I hadn't talked to him in weeks.

When he came upstairs, it took everyone's mind off of the situation, especially mine. He said that he had a break in basic and came home. When he called my house, my sister-in-law told him what was going on, and he came straight to the hospital. We all talked for a while and then went down for lunch.

This was just one of the many times I would learn that the mind can play strange games with you, because as we ate lunch I somehow went back into denial. My mind let me believe that in spite of what I'd seen, my mom was going to be alright. It's the kind of thing you wouldn't believe if it hadn't happened to you.

Everyone else went back upstairs, but my friend Pete, Charisse and I didn't. We said good-bye to my dad and brothers and left, because I wanted to pick up my bag at the airport before it got lost, go home to take a shower, and put on some clean clothes. After doing all of that Pete, Charisse, and I went to the mall where we had all worked so Pete and I could see our friends. In the past, it was where we all could be found most of the time, so we knew that most of them would be there. We stayed at the mall for a while, and one by one many of our friends showed up, and we made plans to go out that night.

Now I know that right about now you have to be thinking, "What is wrong with this guy? His mom is in a hospital in grave condition, and he's making plans to hang out with friends." And I wouldn't blame you, but you have to realize where my head was at the time. I really believed, or wanted to believe, that none of this was happening. When friends saw me and asked how my mom was, I said, "Oh, she's going to be alright." Lest you think that I wasn't all that close to my mom, let me set the record straight. Nothing in my life meant more to me than my mom. She meant the world to me, and we had the best relationship that any mother and son have ever had—EVER ! Looking back a few years later, it was clear that I was not in control of my mind.

After spending some time at the mall, I went back to the hospital to see my family, and I planned to go out afterward. So Charisse, Pete, and three or four other friends went with me to the hospital. It was late when we got there, somewhere around ten o'clock. We were about to go upstairs when a woman at the front desk stopped us. She said we all couldn't go up at one time, so we told her that we were all family and some of us were from out of town. After a few minutes, the woman called upstairs to check. They told her to send us all up.

On the elevator we laughed, thinking she must have believed us and that was why they let us up. When the elevator door opened, the cold reality was right there in front of me. I saw my dad and brothers in the waiting area, and hospital staff were running into my mom's room. A light above her door flashed. I looked at my family and then back at my friends. Not a word needed to be said. We all knew what was going on. I just about sprinted back to the same window that I had been at earlier in the day.. I swear if the window had been open ,I would have jumped out. As I looked outside, I prayed like never before. I was in a daze, and everything seemed so unreal. After some time, I saw people from the hospital talking to my dad. They asked him if he wanted them to send for a priest. I could not believe it. I thought, "No way." My mom was the strongest person I had ever known, and she would beat this. When my dad agreed about the priest, in my head I screamed, "No ! Don't. She'll be alright." You know that kind of scream you see in movies where someone screams and nothing comes out of his mouth? It was like that. A few minutes later they came out and said my mother had passed away.

They let us go in and see her one last time. We all went in and just kind of stood there. To this day I could not tell you if I looked at her or not, and if I did I must have blocked it out, because I have no memory of it at all. I remember going in, but I cannot picture seeing her. We went back into the waiting room, all of us in shock, crying, hugging, and trying to take in what had just happened. After a while, we went home. Again when we got there, we just kind of all looked at each other in disbelief, not knowing what to do next. There was very little if any talking. We just sat or walked around in silence. Having had been up for the better part of two days, I went to bed and slept straight through till morning. I remember that when I woke up, it took just a few seconds until I remembered that my mom was gone.

A few days later, I got a card addressed to me. I knew right away it was from my mom. It had gone to Alabama and been forwarded back to my house. I held it for a while before I could bring myself to open it. The card was like a dozen other cards mom had sent me, the kind you didn't want the other guys in the company to see. They always had puppies or hearts or some such thing and seemed to always come in a pink or purple envelope. Inside she wrote the same as she always had, that she missed me terribly and couldn't wait until I got home. Of course I lost control when I opened and read the card. Imagine getting a card from a loved one, saying how much they missed you, a few days after they died!

The next few weeks went by in the blink of an eye, and then it was time to get back to "normal." I had no normal, but my dad went back to work. My two oldest brothers were married, and my other brother was engaged and still lived at home. But they had jobs and routines to go back to. Being "guys," we didn't really grieve together. Charisse was still in high school, so I was kind of left to deal with this by myself. Don't get me wrong. Charisse was always there for me, and she seemed to know what to say and do when I was down. But we had only been together for less than a year before my mom passed.

For twenty years, I had always gone to my mom for answers to life's tough questions. She would have been the one person who could have gotten me through this, and out the other side, still "normal." Looking back on that time, I shouldn't be too surprised that I came out of it screwed up.

Chapter 3
Mom's Cause of Death

One of the things surrounding my mother's death that has always been hard on me is that, when people ask what the cause of her death was (especially when they learn that she was only fifty-one years old), I don't have an answer for them. When I first heard that she was ill, my brother told me that the doctors didn't know what was wrong with her, and that they were doing tests. Strangely, when I got to the hospital and saw her, it somehow didn't seem to matter. I know that it must sound crazy, but it just didn't even enter my mind. I saw my mom for the first time in over two months, and she was laying there near death. The immediate realization that she was really dying was just so all consuming that it overwhelmed the "how and why."

I would learn later that she had been at an amusement park with my brother's wife and their daughter. They were having a good time when my mother said she wasn't feeling good. A short time later she became very ill. She vomited and lost consciousness. An ambulance took her to the

nearest hospital, where she never regained consciousness. And the hospital was not able to tell
us what caused it. The death certificate gave the
cause of death as something like organ failure,
but didn't list the original cause of her illness.

My brother's wife said that my mom had eat-
en a sandwich before getting sick, and she had
mentioned something about the sandwich tast-
ing bad. But neither the hospital nor the autopsy
mentioned food poisoning. A few months after my
mom's death, my dad and brothers hired an attor-
ney. After a few months of investigating they really
didn't have anything new to go on, but they filed
a lawsuit against the hospital for negligence, because they believed that there were some things
that the hospital failed to do. They also filed a lawsuit against the amusement park for food poisoning because of the sandwich that my mom had
gotten from the park. The attorneys told us that
they really didn't have a case, because the hospital had never checked for food poisoning and
the attorneys' medical expert concluded that the
hospital had not really done anything wrong,. The
medical expert just thought that there were things
the doctors could have done in the diagnostic
process that would have given them a better idea
of what had made her ill. But with the lack of proof
on any of those points, the lawsuits never made it
to court.

For many years, I didn't really give much thought as to the cause of mom's death. Once in a while, if I would be asked why she had passed so young, I would just tell people that as far as we knew it was food poisoning. Although I never believed that this had been the cause, it was just easier to say this than to explain the whole story or to say I didn't know. It wasn't until sometime later that it started to bother me. Charisse and I had two sons, and as they got older I wanted them to know what a very special woman their grandmother had been. I thought that at some point they would ask why she had died, and I wanted them to know the truth. I made a few attempts over the years to try to get the real story, but I always hit a dead end. Also, it was still very painful to remember her passing. After my dad died, I made one last effort to find out. But by then the hospital was gone, as were the records at the coroner's office, and our personal doctor at the time of her death had long since retired.

I have searched the internet and my own memory and have come up with what I believe was the cause of her illness. I can't prove it, but I believe very strongly that a medicine she might have been on at the time was the cause. She suffered from bad arthritis, and a medicine came out about the time of her death for arthritis. This medication was later recalled after it was found to cause bleeding in the stomach, and it caused some deaths.

Her death certificate says that there was hemorrhaging in or of the stomach.

Chapter 4
Things Seemed Normal

Between my mother's death in 1979 and my dad's passing in 2000, my life was pretty normal. Charisse and I were married in 1981, when she was nineteen and I was twenty-two. We had our first son Brandon in 1985. In January of 1988 we bought and moved into our first house, and three weeks later our second son Tyler was born. The next five years were very good ones. I worked at a very nice, upscale restaurant in Cleveland, Ohio. I was the pastry chef. In January of 1989 I went to Paris, France, for one month to attend a culinary school and to work at a hotel there.

I worked at the restaurant until July of 1993, when I was laid off. The economy had gotten bad, and the restaurant was very expensive. Business had dropped way off. Losing that job was really hard on me. Being let go was the last thing that I ever thought would happen. I went for over a year without a job, in part because of the bad economy. In hindsight, it had more to do with anxiety, but I didn't know anything about mental illness then, so I just blamed myself and got very depressed. Eventually, Charisse and I started our own business, and we got back on track. We had had to sell our house the year after I lost my job, and moved to an apartment. In 1998 we were surprised and blessed with the birth of our daughter, Anna. We had to rent a house because our apartment had only two bedrooms.

For all of those years I had my ups and downs, mentally and emotionally. But until I started having panic attacks in 2000, after my father passed, I had no idea what was really happening to me in terms of anxiety, OCD, PTSD, and all the rest of the things I've gone on to experience. I went through those times either feeling like a big loser or just being in denial. Every time I was without a job I had to deal with anxiety or depression or both.

I look back and see so many times when I was racked with anxiety. For example, just a few weeks before I went to Paris, I went to the emergency room, because I thought I was having heart problems. They could not find anything wrong and sent me home. A day or two later I went to my doctor, and he said that the chest pain and difficulty breathing was either acid reflux or anxiety. He prescribed both Zantac and Xanax . Looking back now, I know that I couldn't have made it to and from Paris or survived my time there without the Xanax.

I also look back to times when I was out of work. I would drive around the block of a company at which I was supposed to be applying, and not be able to summon the courage to go in. I would drive home ashamed and depressed, only to repeat it all over a few days or so later. And each time I convinced myself that I could really go through with applying, but I would almost always fail to even pull into the parking lot. I can think back to many, many times when I would get very uncomfortable in social situations. Each time I had any of these experiences it would make it harder and harder to go through it the next time.

But I think the worst part of all of that was not knowing anything about mental and emotional health, and thinking that I was just weak. It really does help to put a name to those problems, and to know that it's something that is pretty much out of your control and that you need help. I really wish that guys would seek and receive help, without putting it off and suffering needlessly. I know that much of our society has placed a stigma on the whole mental health subject. We really need to get past all of the negative perceptions. It would make life easier for millions of people.

Chapter 5
Someone to Lean On

There is an area in which I know that I have been the luckiest man in the world. And that would be with regards to my wife Charisse. It saddens me to know that not everyone who goes through something like this has the support that I had, and continue to have, from my wife. I hope that other guys can find someone, whether a spouse, a friend, or a mental-health professional that they can count on to be there when you really need it most. As I've said elsewhere in this book, Charisse and I have been together for thirty years. And she really can spot changes in my mood and personality even when I don't, and that is very valuable. Because sometimes by the time you notice some changes in yourself, you may be in worse shape.

From the very beginning of our relationship, Charisse has been my rock, whether she knew it or not. When my mom died, Charisse and I had only been dating for eleven months. I was twenty, and she was just turning seventeen. And yet somehow she always said and did just the right things. She somehow always got it.

The summer after my mom passed, Charisse, a mutual friend, and I moved down to Houston. Cleveland was going through a downturn, and Houston was booming. When we got down there, I just fell apart. I learned later that in the rank of traumatic life events, the loss of a loved one, a move to a new place, and the loss of a job are the three worst. And with the move to Houston, I had all three in the span of about nine months. Charisse and our friend did well in Houston. They found jobs and adapted very well. But I found it hard to leave the apartment most days. I got, but never started, a handful of jobs and then just went downhill after awhile. Charisse would sometimes come home from work and find me sitting in a corner crying like a baby. That lasted for a few months until we ran out of money and came home to Cleveland. Through all of it, Charisse was incredible. I can say with little doubt that I never would have gotten through my mother's death or any of the many other problems since without Charisse. And yet somehow she has always made me feel like I was the strong one. I wish every guy going through tough times had a Charisse of his own.

In the language of mental health, Charisse would be referred to as my "safe person." That is to say, I can go places and do things with her by my side that I wouldn't be able to do without her. I am very lucky that she doesn't have a problem with always having to be there when I go pretty much anywhere. I think that the concept of a safe person is actually kind of simple. Just knowing that someone is there with me who knows my little secret takes a lot of the pressure off me. And it's the pressure and fear that is so debilitating. I don't really expect her to do anything. Just being there is all I need. But that's not to say that anyone could be my safe person. I don't tell most people I know about my problem, so they couldn't help like Charisse does. In fact, they would put more pressure on me because, God forbid that I start to panic in front of family or friends and have them find out that I am not "normal."

Your safe person can't be a pushover, though. You need her to test you and push you sometimes. She needs to know when to give you a hand up or a pat on the back. I wish you the best of luck finding your safe person. It would be really hard to go through this alone.

Chapter 6
Fast Forward to 2000

My Dad's health had been in a gradual decline. I just assumed it was part of his aging. He was 74 years old and had dealt with a handful of medical issues over the last ten to fifteen years. The big ones being two bypass surgeries and prostate cancer. In early 2000 his health seemed to be more of an issue than ever. He was hospitalized for three or four days. His doctor had ordered some tests but couldn't put his finger on what was causing his problems. And being in the hospital at this point in his life really aggravated him, So now he was feeling bad physically and mentally as well. They sent him home and his doctor was going to follow up with various outpatient tests. By Easter he was getting worse, he was having digestive problems and had just about stopped eating and was getting weaker by the day. I remember taking him some home made soup (beef barley, one of his favorites) and he wouldn't even try to eat it. When he had tried to eat he would just get stomach pains and wasn't able to have normal bowel movements. He didn't want to go back to the hospital. He had enough and didn't feel like going through all the testing and other stuff anymore. After a lot of begging and bugging we were able to convince him to go to the hospital. The first few days were like his time in the hospital just a few months before, test after test and still no good answers as to what was wrong with him. Then a surgeon said the problem was my Dad's gallbladder and he needed to have it removed immediately (this was on a Fri.) My Dad's doctor said no to the surgery because he was concerned that my Dad wouldn't make it through the surgery. So the two doctors went back and forth over the weekend on whether to have surgery or not. By Monday it became apparent that there was no choice but to do the surgery. Dad agreed to have it done and they took him down to get ready for the operation. The surgeon got the family together to let us know my Dad was very weak and may not make it through the operation.He said he would go as fast as he could and do everything he could to ease the burden on my Dad's body. He also said the surgery would take several hours.

After seeing Dad one more time and telling him we loved him they took him in and we (my Dads wife, Lora, my brothers and our families) went downstairs to the cafeteria to grab a little something to eat and wait it out. After just over an hour someone came looking for us and told us that the surgeon wanted to see us back upstairs.

Of course our first thoughts were that he didn't make it through the operation as they had feared he might not. There were about 7 or 8 of us and they took us to a small room to wait for the surgeon. The surgeon came in and explained that when they went into my Dad's abdomen they found that his organs were covered with very tiny tumors, he compared it to sand on a beach, and that they hadn't shown up on x-rays or CT scans because they were so small. He told us that they just closed my Dad back up, as it didn't make any sense to remove the gallbladder. He then said that he would not recommend putting my Dad through the normal cancer treatment, saying it wouldn't help and would just make him sicker and would take away from whatever quality of life my Dad had left. He felt that my Dad had about 6 months to a year to live, and would know more in a few days when they got results back from the biopsy on some samples they had taken. He also recommended not telling my Dad about the tumors, sighting patients whose health declined very fast after being told as opposed to others who did better not knowing.

Over the next few days I wrestled with the fact that my Dad had only months to live. It was just starting to sink in when we were called to the hospital to go over the results of the biopsy. The surgeon told us that my Dad's cancer was worse than he had thought, it turned out to be pancreatic cancer and that the prognosis was that my Dad probably only had weeks to live. WOW, just when I was coming to grips with the idea of months now we were down to weeks. And the news just went down hill from there, as the doctor recommended that we take Dad home so he could "enjoy" his remaining time at home and not in a hospital. None of us said a word. We felt that taking him home would just speed things up, because we felt that the IV's and meds were all that were keeping him going. I remember thinking that no way in hell were we taking him home and shorten what time we had left with him, and as long as he was in the hospital they could keep him going longer and we wanted every day we could get. But over the next week I could see how miserable he was in the hospital and it was clear that the right thing to do was to let him go home where he would be happier. At the same point it seemed like Lora and my brothers and I all came to that conclusion and were in total agreement that he should go home.

He went home on Saturday afternoon and I didn't go to see him that day as I thought that the trip home would most likely be tough on him and we would just let him rest. When we (Charisse, Brandon, Tyler, Anna and I) went to see him the next day he looked better than he had in weeks. That let me know that bringing him home was the right thing to do. But seeing him look so good started me feeling like maybe he could keep going for months or even a year. That hope came crashing down the very next day, when we went to see him he was bad again. Over the next few days I prayed every time I saw him and every night that God would work some kind of miracle and he would get better. That Thursday when I went to see him he was worse yet, he was in a great deal of pain and would not take his pain medications. He had been throwing up and thought that the medications were causing it. We knew it wasn't but we couldn't tell him that it was because he was dying, although he must have known that anyway. In frustration I lost it and just screamed at him to take the medicine. I could not stand to see him in that kind of pain. He was the toughest guy I had ever known and could deal with pain so I knew he was really hurting. He looked at me and said OK and took the pain killers. I left after that, I was by myself and didn't think I would make it home. It was really hitting home that my Dad was dying and would most likely not last more than a day or two. It was not easy to watch my hero, my superman slip away like that. By now he was skin and bones and couldn't get out of the bed he was in, a hospital bed in his living room. This was the strongest, toughest man I had ever known and he could hardly move a muscle. The next day he seemed in good spirits , he was in less pain, but he was starting to slip mentally. He started telling me that the night before he had gone out to the kitchen and made himself some fried bologna (one of his favorite things to eat). He went into great detail about how he had sliced the onions and fried them then added the bologna and ketchup and cooked it all together. He said to me "Dino I ate the hell out of it, and it was great". He had such a smile on his face I believe he could taste the fried bologna. He also had started to see things that weren't there, something about a face in his ceiling fan and a boy with a pony. He dosed off after that and to my total amazement, I had gotten to a place mentally where I started praying to God, my Mom and all of my father's deceased relatives to please come and take him over with them so he would be at peace. If someone had told me just a few days earlier that I would be praying for my fathers passing, I wouldn't have believed it. But it felt so right, it was time and I knew it. When we went back on Saturday he was all but gone, he didn't respond to anything, he didn't blink or move at all. We only stayed for a few minutes, I just could not take seeing him like that. When we left I pretty much knew that it would be the last time I would see him.

Later at home while we were eating dinner the phone rang and one of my sons saw on the caller ID that it was from my Dad's house. I came completely unglued, and started yelling not to answer it and when Charisse answered it, I said I didn't want to talk to anyone. Charisse stepped into another room as she talked to my brother Jim on the phone and I started to scream for her to hang up. I was totally losing it, our boys were just looking at me like "what's up with him". Of course I thought Jim was calling to tell us that Dad had passed and even though I thought I was ready for it , I wasn't even close. Jim had called to touch base with us and say my Dad's condition had not changed. Later that evening Charisse and the kids were asleep, it was only about 10:00 or 10:30 pm. But we were all really tired we had been through over thirty straight days of ups and downs and were drained. I got down on my knees at the side of my bed to pray as I did each night. I had a two part prayer and in the middle I would pray about things that had happened that day or were on my mind that day. I was at that middle part, praying again for God, my Mom and other relatives to help my Dad pass. No sooner had I finished then the phone rang. I knew it would be someone calling to tell us that Dad had passed, it was my brother Rick, he said my Dad had passed just a few minutes earlier. It was strange that just a few hours earlier I freaked out when my other brother, Jim called and now I was at peace knowing that he had gone to be with his deceased loved ones.

Later that night it struck me out of nowhere that I was parentless. It's kind of crazy, but even at forty-one years old that was really unsettling,

36

knowing that both of the people who brought me into this world and loved and cared for me were gone. It made me feel so alone and lost.

Chapter 7
What's Happening ?

During the last month or so of my dad's life, things got stressful, with trips to either the hospital or my dad's house every day. Because of what I would later recognize as OCD, I had my family on a pretty structured schedule. I don't mean that I was controlling. But I have always liked to have a routine and didn't (and still don't) like surprises or disruptions. So every day our sons would get home at the same time, have a snack and do their homework. We ate dinner at 5:30 p.m., every day, and the kids would go to bed at the same time each night.

Previously, my wife and I had run our own catering business . But shortly after our daughter was born in 1998, we decided that I would stay home with our daughter, and my wife would continue the business. So by this time I had been staying home with my daughter for a little over a year, and I structured our day, just like I had everything else. It really was pretty nice. She would wake up every day at the same time almost like clockwork. She would eat, and we would play all morning. Then she would take her nap at the usual time, wake up at the usual time, and eat lunch. We would play or read or watch TV until my wife came home. We only had one car so my daughter and I were stuck at home all day. But I didn't mind it that much. The time went by pretty quickly each day.

Now under normal conditions, having this kind of structure was just fine with me. But once my dad got sick, there were no normal conditions for about a month. And when you are that structured for as long as we had been, then suddenly everything changes, you're in for trouble. As I said, all five of us would go to see him every day. We would leave as soon as the boys got home from school and had a snack. We would go to the hospital for a few hours, and that's no picnic with a girl not quite two years old and boys fifteen and twelve years old. Anna, our daughter, was especially hard to keep happy for that long in a hospital. If we put her down she would get into trouble or try to run off.

Our new schedule also meant no more eating dinner at 5:30 pm. or even at home. Most of the time we stopped on our way home, got fast food, and went home to eat. This meant getting the kids a snack at the hospital, but we didn't want to spend our whole visit in the cafeteria, so that required feeding the kids from a vending machine. There aren't many good choices in vending machines. In the evening when we got home with our takeout, the boys would have to eat, do their homework, and go to bed. You can keep this kind of schedule for a day or two, but every day for over three weeks really took its toll on all of us. Added to that, watching my father's health get worse day by day meant I was at the end of my rope.

For those last two weeks or so I was constantly stressed. I would catch myself with my jaw clenched all the time. I was very irritable and on edge 24/7. I couldn't sleep and wasn't really eating. I drank Pepsi or Coke all day, because I needed the caffeine, but it wasn't helping me cope with the stress. I jumped at the slightest noise. Anything at all, the phone or one of the kids screaming, was too much. And I was being rough on our children. It seemed like everything they did made me mad, and I would start yelling.

I hated how I was behaving, but I expected it to stop after my dad passed. But it didn't. It didn't even let up at all. I was starting to worry about it, but I hoped it would just go away. Even though things were back to normal, in terms of our schedule, I just couldn't bring myself down. At the time I described it to my wife as feeling like a switch had been turned on in me, and I had no idea how to shut it off. I felt I was always "on."

It all came to a head about three or four weeks after my dad passed. The boys were out of school for summer vacation, and we went bowling. It was actually a pretty good time. We had the whole place to ourselves, and Anna was able to run around and not get into any trouble. Well, my father-in-law heard about our outing and said he'd like to take us bowling. So a few days later we all went, but this time when we walked into the bowling alley, it was packed. We didn't want to disappoint my father in-law so we stayed. I wasn't thrilled because I was still stressed out and hated crowds, so that made it worse. The boys weren't happy because there were a lot of teenagers there, and the boys really weren't very good at bowling. As for my daughter, Anna wanted to run around, but the place was so crowded. On top of that, people were having a birthday party for their child, and all the balloons and party stuff was like a magnet for Anna. She kept going over and trying to get anything she could get her hands on, and the people weren't thrilled with her. So I really started to freak out inside and just wanted to get the hell out of there.

All of a sudden, it hit me: my first panic attack!

I had never felt anything like it in my life. I don't really recall the order the symptoms came in, but I do remember that they arrived one at a time, one right over the other, piling up and magnifying with each second. There was sweating, a lightheaded feeling, dizziness, a rapid heartbeat, a shortness of breath, and a tightness in my chest. Also, I felt hot all over, and I had the feeling of being out of control both mentally and physically. It seemed to be in slow motion, and it felt like I wasn't there but was watching it happen from a few feet away. Luckily everyone was done bowling and was ready to go. My father in-law drove that day, thank God!

I climbed into the back of his minivan and held on all the way home. I hadn't told anyone, not even my wife. I didn't think I could even explain what was happening, nor could I really do anything but ride out whatever this was. By the time we got home, I was starting to feel better. I took my wife into another room and told her what had happened, and that seemed to help. We decided that I had suffered a panic or anxiety attack, and I would go to the doctor the very next day.

All that night, I just waited for it to happen again. It never did return that night, but I was pretty stressed and didn't sleep much. We had talked about me going to the doctor for a week or two before the panic attack, but I kept putting it off. Now I was scared as hell, so I was ready to get checked out, as there was a part of me that thought it might have been a physical problem and not mental. The next day we made an appointment but couldn't get in to see the doctor for a couple of days.

Oddly, when the day came to see him, I started to have really bad anxiety. As my wife drove us there, I told her that I couldn't go through with the appointment. Luckily for me, Charisse wasn't going to turn back no matter what I said. That was just the first of many times over the years that she would talk me into doing what she knew was best for me, in spite of me trying to talk my way out of whatever it was. I have been so blessed to have her at my side throughout this whole time.

When the doctor came in , he asked what I was there for, and I just broke down sobbing. It lasted for a few minutes, so Charisse had to tell him what was going on. The crying actually made me feel better and less stressed than I had in a long time. After telling the doctor what had been happening, and that I had lost my dad, he explained about anxiety and panic attacks. He prescribed Paxil and Xanax for me. On the way home, I felt better than I had in quite awhile. We got the meds, and I started on them.

I know that a lot of doctors do not like to prescribe Xanax, and I understand why. But for the eight years I have been on meds, that little pill has been a lifesaver. I suppose that some doctors wouldn't be happy that I have come to need it like I do, but I have used it over the years for help sleeping and to get me through times that I wouldn't have been able to get through without it. I have certainly never abused it, but I do know that it would be very hard to live without it. So in that sense I guess I am dependent on it, but that's the way it has to be for now.

Chapter 8
Treatment

After my first panic attack, getting treatment, especially of the pharmaceutical kind, was a no brainer. The mental and physical feelings were just way too strong and very scary. I was very relieved that I had been prescribed medication. It was important to know that I was getting meds that I felt would keep panic attacks at bay or at least lessen their strength. In spite of the fact that I have never liked the idea of taking prescription medicine, I knew that I had no ability to fight the panic attacks without meds.

The Paxil was an everyday med, and the Xanax was for dealing with panic. I didn't expect the side effects I got from the Paxil. After taking the first one or two doses, I couldn't stand up without becoming extremely dizzy. This got worse with each dose. It got to the point where I just couldn't take it, and I stopped the Paxil on my own without checking with the doctor first, which was not a smart thing to do. The dizziness just got worse. My wife called the doctor, and he said I shouldn't have quit the Paxil, and he said to go right back on it. So instead of having side effects for three days or so, my stopping and starting stretched the side effects out for about a week. After the side effects stopped, I did OK. I stayed on the Paxil for over two years. And during that time I argued with my doctor over whether or not the Paxil was responsible for my gaining over thirty pounds in a little over a year. I believed then and still believe that the Paxil did indeed cause my weight gain. At about two years or so, it seemed that the Paxil was not working anymore. But because I had endured such a hard time getting on the it, I did not want to go through the side effects of getting off Paxil and then on a new drug. So I put off going to the doctor to switch for a good while.

At that time, I decided to seek professional help, so my doctor give me the names of a few psychologists. It was difficult to take this step. Going to a total stranger and telling him about my problems was not very appealing to me. And as I would find out, you may have to go to more than one until you find the right fit. I went to my first psychologist three or four times before deciding that she wasn't a good fit for me. So I had to start the process over again. While seeing the first counselor, I found out that she could not prescribe meds, and I needed to get them from a psychiatrist. So my first counselor referred me to a psychiatrist, and I had to go to her and tell her my whole story. She prescribed a different med, after telling me that we may have to try different drugs and maybe different combinations to get the right fit for me. So I got my new meds and sought out a new psychologist. And God smiled down on me, and I found a wonderful psychologist. Dr. Green was an angel. I felt so comfortable from the moment I walked into her office.

I saw Dr. Green for almost a year, and she was awesome. She was so easy to talk to, and very understanding. Unfortunately, she found out that she had cancer, and she had to give up her practice. She recommended another counselor in her office. She knew it was going to be hard for me to start over with someone new, so she told me to think about it for a little while. It was really hard to consider going to anyone but Dr. Green, so I put off making a decision for a while. Then I decided that I would try again on my own, with the help of books and the internet, to treat myself. That didn't work so well. Finally, after months of regressing, I heard my wife say, "You have an appointment next week with a new counselor." She had given me enough time and seen me get worse instead of better. She knew, even if I didn't, that it was time to go back to a professional. I didn't fight it at all because I'd known for a while that I was just getting worse.

The appointment was with a counselor named Lisa, and she was part of the same office as Dr. Green, so at least the surroundings would be familiar. Someone must have been looking out for me because Lisa was great. She was a lot like Dr. Green.

My wife came with me for my appointments, She would drive me, because I would get too nervous before an appointment and couldn't drive myself. Although I could have done the appointment alone, Charisse and I had been married for almost twenty-five years at that point, and she really did know me better than I knew myself. She can see changes in me before I even notice them myself. So she was, and is, a great help to me as I try to get back to "normal."

And you may have noticed a pattern with the doctors: they were all females. This is just one of the things that I felt other men might relate to. There was no way I was going to another guy and talking about my problems and, yes, crying in front of him. I haven't taken a poll but I would bet on it that most men would say the exact same thing about the gender of their counselor.

I know that I would not have opened up as much to a male doctor as I have to Dr. Green and Lisa. It may sound stupid, but you know the old saying: "Big boys don't cry." Guys always have to keep their guard up with other guys.

Chapter 9
Day to Day

This chapter describes what life has been like as an agoraphobic person. I think it might be worth saying again. What I've had and still continue to experience is just that: my experience. I have never spoken to another agoraphobic, and I have not read any specific first-hand accounts from one either. This is exactly what led me to write this book in the first place.

Now if you or a close family member or friend have not had to deal with this condition, then you might think, "What's so special about the kind of day that the author is writing about?"

And you would be correct, and that's the point. There is nothing special about an agoraphobic's day. They are generally all the same and not at all that exciting.

In addition to agoraphobia, I also have obsessive-compulsive disorder, which for better or worse has kept me very regimented in my day-to-day life. I am up at pretty much the same time every day, which is in part due to not being able to sleep. In five years I don't think I have had more than a two dozen nights of good sleep. Breakfast has been the same, literally, for at least five or six years. I have whole-grain cereal, fenugreek tea, and a glass of grape juice. Breakfast is at around 8:00 a.m. each weekday. Lunch is between 12:00 p.m. to 12:30 p.m. It has consisted of two or three pieces of whole-grain toast with honey, one apple, and a cup of green tea for just as many years as my breakfast has. At dinner I eat whatever the rest of my family is having. I believe that eating the same thing at the same time each day is the result of the OCD in two ways. One is just the function of the OCD itself (i.e., not wanting to deviate from a consistent pattern for fear of the unknown). The other is an indirect result of the OCD in that I am obsessed with the idea that I am at a high risk for a heart attack, even though there is no medical reason to believe this might be the case. However, with the OCD, I obsess about the things that scare me most and those things over which I feel that I have little or no control.

I am fortunately able to make myself useful to my family by cleaning, doing laundry, cooking, and being at home with my daughter after school and during vacations, such as summer and other holidays. We lived in a series of rentals with no outside yard work and then bought a condo with no outside maintenance, so that saved me from having to go out. If I went out, I might encounter a neighbor, which scares me way too much. My fear is that any conversation will lead to me being asked what I do for a living or where I work. And how would I explain being home all day, every day? So each day consists of me at home, pretty much doing the same thing and trying not to be seen. I even close the shades if I think there is any chance of being seen. Generally, my time is spent in one of three ways: reading the newspaper, watching television, or going online. I mostly study politics, world news, and social causes, like the environment or war in Iraq, among other things. I have signed up for many email newsletters and email actions, like sending messages to politicians and corporate executives. It gives me some sense of still being involved with the rest of society. But it leaves me yelling at the television a lot.

One thing that I, and others like me, have to contend with is downtime. These are large blocks of time with nothing to do and very little, if anything, worthwhile to think about. My grandmother used to say "An idle mind is the devil's playground." Too much downtime almost always turns into a time for negative THINKING. And more likely than not, that time will be used to reinforce how depressed, hopeless, and pessimistic I feel about myself and my situation. So it's very important to keep busy and stay as upbeat as you can.

Early in my therapy, my psychologist repeatedly tried to get me to think in terms of small steps.

An example of this is to start going out to the mailbox at the end of my driveway each day for the mail. I remember thinking how pathetic I felt that something so simple could be a real accomplishment for me. But I tried to keep a positive outlook and did it anyway. After three or four days I really did feel good about being able to go for the mail. I have to admit, though, that after hearing the "atta boy" from my wife and the psychologist, I really was torn between crying or feeling pretty good about myself.

Every day, every week, and every month were and are full of many, many of those and other highs and lows and successes and failures.

Chapter 10
How Much Information and to Whom?

I have found that I really have to weigh heavily whom I tell about my situation and how much I tell them. It is an ongoing process. Sometimes you have a while to consider all the options, and other times you have to make very quick decisions. I have had different levels of disclosure with the people in my life, whether it's family, friends, or other people I had to interact with. At the top is, of course, my wife, who is my safe person. She gets it all, the good, the bad, and the really ugly.

My children are a different story. And I would imagine that this is an area where men dealing with agoraphobia will find common ground. I have two sons who, as of this writing, are twenty-three and twenty-six . I also have a daughter who, as of this writing, is twelve . There are any number of ways to look at each of them. Gender plays a role, as does age, as does the fact that I had a father who was "Superman" and who seemed indestructible. I likewise wanted to be a strong example to my sons. That has been one of the really tough things that I have had to deal with these last six years or so. How can you appear strong when you're afraid to leave the house? How can you be the bread winner, head of the household when you can't go to work? How do you explain that dad doesn't leave the house, except for an "appointment"? What do you say to your child when they are ten or twelve, fourteen, sixteen, eighteen, or twenty? How do you tell them to be brave and not to worry about speaking in front of a class at school, or taking a driving lesson or test? It's tough to give them encouragement to do something that I know I can't do, and they may even know that I can't do it. My sons have grown into really good young men. So I guess that my mental issues have had only a very little impact on their lives . I just could never in all these years imagine sitting them down and telling them just how bad my condition was. I know that I would have been very uncomfortable and am fairly sure they would have too. This is one of the main reasons why I think so many veterans returning from Iraq and Afghanistan have such a hard time. Most guys just have such a hard time letting down their guard and showing a perceived weakness. I hope that my book and/or the website I plan to start after my book is published will be of help to them. If it at least gets them to trust just one person they can open up to, that would be a good start. They need to know that telling their story is so helpful, it's such a release , and lifts the weight off of them, rather then carry that burden all by themselves and in effect hiding their true condition .

I have three older brothers who, when we were kids, taught me I had to be tough to get by. I was regularly on the receiving end of some brotherly fights when I was young. So how do I let them in on what I am going through? How do I show weakness to the same guys who I wouldn't let know that their punches and hits really hurt? So I have never talked about my condition to any of them. I know they know I have some kind of mental/emotional issues. But I don't believe they have any idea just how bad I get at times.

I go through the same kind of thought processes with extended family and friends as well. In almost all cases, I found the less I said the better. Unfortunately, mental illness is not accepted that well. I feel I have to keep reminding you, the reader, that I don't have answers to a lot of these questions. But I hope that hearing my story will allow you to see that others are going through much of the same things while dealing with anxiety and agoraphobia. I have spent a lot of time thinking that I was the only one like me in the world. I think that if I had heard the experiences of other guys like me, it would have made this all a little easier to deal with. I would have known that I wasn't the freak I thought I was.

I have one last thing to say on this topic. There have been times when I was at an event or in a room with family and friends who I knew were aware of my condition. And it was strange because I knew they knew, and they knew I was aware they knew, and somehow it took a lot of the pressure off of me and made it much easier to get through the evening, or day, or whatever. And the funny thing is that even though everyone knew about my condition, it was never brought up. We all just acted like everything was normal.

Chapter 11
Time

Time is something we all think about. In one way or another, time is truly a constant in everyone's life. Songs are written about it, and books are written about it. Some people have very little time to do all that they have to do, while others get bored because they have too much time on their hands. You often hear people complain that something took too long. Others complain that something, let's say a movie or a day at the beach, went by way too fast. And yet in reality, every minute is one minute long, every hour is sixty minutes long, and every day is twenty-four hours long. So it's really our perception of time that slows down or speeds up, causing stress and anxiety.

I bring up time because I have dealt with agoraphobia for all these years, and I have found that for me, time is almost always the enemy. And by time I mean across the board—seconds, minutes, hours, days, months, and years—all seem to make my life harder in one way or another. I can usually deal with minutes and hours. Some are faster, and some are slower. But the days, weeks, and months just fly by, leaving me wondering where in the hell did they go. Even as I write this, I am amazed and embarrassed that I have been dealing with the problem of agoraphobia for so dammed long. Even today, as I am writing this, I am hating myself and feeling somewhat worthless in that I should have beaten this by now.

Everyone is different, and I hope that you or your loved one don't travel down the same path that I have. I've allowed myself to fall into a cycle of ups and downs, highs and lows, and starts and stops. I have gotten too excited sometimes and thought that I had this illness beat, and then when I have a setback, it leads to the lowest of lows. Living in northeast Ohio, I have also fallen into seasonal highs and lows as summer changes into fall, and fall into winter, and winter into spring.

Another aspect of time, which might be the worst, is dealing with expectations. Over the years, I have unfortunately got caught up in a cycle of denial and acceptance. And that has lead to great frustration, self-doubt, and self-loathing. When I look at all the time I've had over the last six years, I am really hard on myself that I didn't do something constructive with the time. There are so many things that I would have liked to have done. I could have learned another language or learned to play a musical instrument. I could have written this book and maybe others. I could have taken online college courses and gotten a degree in something. I have had an interest in genealogy for a number of years and could have done much more work on my family and my wife's family.

Now you might be thinking, "Well then, why didn't you do all or some of those things?" And I'd say, "Good question!" The answer is not a simple one, but is wrapped up in the mess that is agoraphobia, obsessive-compulsive disorder, depression, anxiety, fear, and a misunderstanding of all of the above. You see, I could and did convince myself that mental wellness was just over the horizon, and if I started a long-term project I either wouldn't finish it or I would have to admit that getting through this was going to take longer than I wanted to believed. You go through thinking that you have a handle on the condition one minute, to feeling hopeless and thinking that you might never get back to "normal." I have not learned or been able to wrap my mind around the idea that this is a project that is to be taken in steps. It is not simply waking up one day and being cured. And even after all these years, and being told at one of my very first sessions with my psychologist that I needed to think of progress in terms of baby steps, something in my DNA just blocks that message from getting through. Maybe there is just something about the phrase "mental illness" that I just don't get. If my problem were some physical illness, and I was told it would take at least six months to heal or get over, I wouldn't start questioning my progress after one month.

It's almost like I'm in a chess game with myself, and the only way to lose is to try to out think yourself.

Chapter 12
Money

Seriously, there almost isn't a need to explain money in the context of this book. When you can't leave the house, it's difficult, if not impossible, to earn a living. And I must stop here to apologize to women who may be reading, but this is another area that I think men have a harder time dealing with than women do. And of course, I am speaking only about my belief and from my experience and upbringing.

My generation of men had fathers who served in World War II, or whose parents or grandparents went through the Great Depression. A son raised in the 1960s and 1970s is more likely to have had a dad who worked and a mother who was a "housewife," or as in my case, a mother who worked full time after the youngest child had started school. Nevertheless, dad was the breadwinner and the head of the household. He was the "wait until your father gets home" guy. During that time, when the economy was heavily manufacturing driven, my father was like most of the fathers in the neighborhood. He was a factory worker. Even from an early age, I was aware of how hard he worked. We had been to his factory many times, and it was not all that pleasant of a place. It was very noisy and very hot, with blast furnaces all around. It smelled of what I would realize much later were nasty chemicals. It was the kind of smell that would come home with my dad on his uniform.

Dad worked thirty-four years in the same factory, rarely missing a day of work. My mother worked third-shift in the factory right across from my dad's, then came home and did all that any mother had to do in those days, such as shopping, cooking, and keeping the kids out of trouble. So when you have parents like mine as your role models, you learn what a big responsibility it is to be there to provide for your family.

You also learn the importance of setting a positive example. And until I started having trouble, I was proud to have been that kind of parent. I did everything it took to provide for my family, even insisting that my wife stay home with our boys as my mom had with my brothers and me. I felt especially proud that I could bring in enough income so that we could live a good life on just my salary. And as my sons got older, it was important for me to provide that "strong role model" for them.

So it became very difficult to deal with it when my agoraphobia made it virtually impossible to leave the house. And as I sank farther and farther into my own little world, and as my wife had to take on more and more of what had been my responsibilities, the less I thought of myself as a person, a father, and as a husband. And yes, the thought that they didn't need me or might be better off without me started to creep into my head.

At some point when money became very tight, and it was tougher every day for my wife to make ends meet, she brought up the idea of trying to get social security disability. I know that it was very hard for her to ask, and that she wouldn't have done so if it wasn't an absolute necessity. But now I had let my wife down, I wasn't providing for my family, and I had gotten so bad that I might qualify for social security disability. Boy, did I feel worthless. Then came the thought that even though I wanted no part of collecting disability, I knew it wasn't fair to dismiss it and leave my family hanging. So the dilemma was to admit that I was so bad off mentally that it made sense to try for disability, or to deny the cold, hard facts and put my family in real financial trouble. After a few days of thinking about it, I agreed to try, even though a part of me was hoping I would not qualify. Luckily, I was able to apply without having to go in person, as I don't know if I could have sat and told someone I didn't know about my problems, when their job was to approve or deny my claim.

At first I was denied and had to have my psychologist write a letter to the Social Security Disability Administration. I also wrote a letter to them explaining just how important it was for me to bring some money into the house, even by these means. Thankfully, they accepted my claim. And it was hard to decide whether to be happy or really depressed that I had been accepted. In the long run, it was truly a blessing to have gotten that money. Even if I wasn't "earning" an income, I was helping to pay the bills.

Now with all that being said, there are downsides to collecting disability. One is that I never wanted anyone to know, not even my children, because I would be embarrassed or ashamed. The other downside is that just like drugs, you can become addicted to, and dependent on, that flow of money. And in a way it can hold you back, by taking the pressure off you to conquer your illness. You keep putting it off until "tomorrow." So as with medication, you have to use caution and probably be under someone's watch and care. Like anything else, it is a tool, and if used right it can be of great help.

Chapter 13
Regrets

Regrets—you can't live with them, you can't live without them. I know the subject of regrets has been mentioned in other places in this book, but I believe that they should have their own chapter. I have talked about regretting some things, like having nothing really to show for all this time that I have been trapped at home. That is a huge regret, and there are others as well. But almost nothing compares to my regrets when it comes to my immediate family.

I think about all the times that I stayed home while my wife and children went to events, like school plays and music events. I have missed so many school-related events that I could never count all of them. I have missed many, many holidays as well. I missed Christmas at my father in-law's house for a number of consecutive years. I've missed many meals out at restaurants, sometimes for special occasions and other times just for a dinner out. I've missed cookouts and outings in the park.

I even missed my second son's graduation from high school. I was lucky that he had two ceremonies, one for his vocational school that was small, which I went to. But the one for his actual high school was much larger and at a big auditorium in downtown Cleveland, which I didn't go to. I missed my brother's second wedding.

And just to be accurate, when I say "missed," I simply mean I could not bring myself to go to these events, because I allowed fear of the unknown to take over and override my common sense and rational thoughts. And not only is that an enormous regret, but every time I allowed my fear to take over, I sank deeper and deeper into the trap that is agoraphobia. And when the next event came up, it was harder than the one before to seriously consider going, because now I had set these earlier precedents. Instead of just this one hurdle, I had all the other hurdles that I had set out before. That, in itself, is one of my big mistakes. Instead of looking at each situation as a separate event, to be weighed on its own as to the things I would fear and those things that I might be able to deal with, I allowed myself to pretty much place equal weight on every event. No matter how big or small, how short or long in duration, in my mind they each had just about the same amount of fear and pressure.

And in closing on the subject of regrets, I would have to say that my biggest regret is missing the milestone moments in my daughter's life to this point. So many times she would come home and say, "Daddy, you should have seen me swim" or "I climbed on the monkey bars at the park" or "You should have seen how fast I ran when I was racing my friend." It's tough enough that I missed those wonderful moments, but it's so much tougher that she missed me at those very special times. That is one of the things that becomes easy to forget when you're caught up in your own little world and are thinking about yourself and from your perspective. But when you stop and think about how your condition affects the lives of those around you, it really hits you like a sucker punch.

It's hard to get up from that one.

With all of that said, in terms of regrets, I also know that in many ways I have been extremely fortunate. Take the death of my parents, for instance. Many people have to deal with guilt and regrets because they had strained relationships with a loved one when that loved one passes. Or people live with losing someone and having many things that they regret they had, or had not, said to their loved one, and then it's too late. My mother and I had an outstanding relationship. I was in basic training when she became ill, but we had written each other and spoken on the phone many times under those circumstances, which was the first time I had been away from home. You say things in cards and letters that you might not say in person. These are things like "I love you" and "I really miss you." With my dad, I was lucky, because when

I was younger he was very much the disciplinarian and always seemed to be afraid to get too close, so he could maintain a little bit of that fear factor. But once I became an adult, our relationship got much closer, and the older we both got, the closer we became. And at the time of his death, I both loved and respected him very much. Also, because his death came much slower than my mom's, I was able to take it in and be a little more comfortable knowing that he had lived a good, long life and that he was deeply loved.

Chapter 14
The ABCs of Mental Health

Dealing with my emotional problems has been quite an education. I can talk about PTSD, OCD, SAD (social-anxiety disorder), and agoraphobia with the best of them. I have only half-jokingly thought about taking some classes and becoming a counselor or even a psychologist. Maybe I'll see how this book does, and if I find it helps people, then maybe I'll do it.

They say that there is a fine line between genius and insanity, and I think the same is true for obsessive-compulsive behavior and being organized. As with many things in life, I have found having OCD to be both good and bad.

The bad side is the obvious: the obsessive thinking and negative thoughts. On both the good and bad sides is that even though I have been isolated for many hours each day all these years, the fact that I have a schedule that I stick to (obsessively) has made the time much more bearable than if I just sat and stared at the walls all day. Even if, in the end, they are really about the same thing.

When I say I have a schedule, I mean that being obsessive, which I prefer to think of as being organized, means that I have set my time up so that each day I have things to do at very specific times. I stick to the schedule each day as if I were working or doing something of real importance, which I suppose you could say about the housework I do each day. I feel lucky that my OCD is not as bad as it could be. I have heard and read about people whose lives are totally controlled by their OCD. My experience with OCD has been fairly limited. Mostly, I am concerned with neatness and organization. For example, I hang and fold my clothes in a certain way. On the occasions when my wife does laundry, I will refold my clothes, because she doesn't do it the same way I do. I spend a little bit of time reorganizing the dishes in the dishwasher, because I like them a certain way. I sometimes recheck the doors to make sure they are locked before I go to bed. Because I have children, I have on occasion had to get over some compulsions, because they just weren't worth the stress of always being on the kids to do things a certain way. Plus, I didn't want them to think I was crazy.

In terms of the obsessive thinking, I have found it incredible that the obsessive-compulsive side of your brain can so totally override the rational part. It has been a source of great frustration to do battle with irrational thoughts and lose almost every time. The number of times that the OCD side has convinced the other side of my brain that I was having a heart attack, or that some negative thing was going to happen if I left the house, is mind boggling. It happens almost on a daily basis. Given that, I would have to say that OCD is a curse.

In terms of PTSD, that's a tough one. PTSD is in the news and on the mind of most Americans, because of the young vets coming back from Iraq and Afghanistan who suffer from this disorder. I sometimes feel undeserving to say that I was diagnosed with PTSD, because I am not a war vet, and I actually had a friend question how I could have it. He said, "You weren't in a war." I can't begin to comprehend the hell that these vets went through. To know that every minute could be your last and to always have to be on guard, that stress over months must be horrific.

But the trauma of PTSD can be from many sources. I won't try to define trauma as it pertains to post-traumatic stress disorder. I'll leave that for the professionals. As I have written earlier in this book, my trauma came from the sudden, unexpected death of a loved one, and the helplessness of going through that loss. I also have deep regret and guilt about how I reacted at that time.

As I have written, I only went into her hospital room one time and only for a few minutes. Also, during that time I could not look at, speak to, or touch her. Those feelings were made much clearer to me when my father was dying, and I could see how important it was to talk to and kiss him, and to take in the reality that he was indeed dying. So many times I have wished that I had spoken to my mother. So many times I have wished I had held her hand. So many times I have wished that I would have stayed by her side for all of the time that she had left.

In the years gone by, so many times I have seen on TV, whether real life or on a drama, that someone would talk to their loved one, and the person would just wake up from their coma. I saw on a news report that a person in a coma said she could hear every word that her family said, and that it kept her going and helped her recover. I can't count how many times I have thought, "What if I had talked and touched my mom? Could that have brought her back?" Now I know that it most likely would not have saved her life. But there is always that doubt, and there are times when I can't stand the thought that I didn't do all that I could have for a mother who meant the world to me. Then there is the regret that I didn't spend every minute she had left with her, by her side. Could that have eased the pain of losing her even just a little? Would it have helped to have had those last few hours to let it sink in that my mother was really dying? And would I not have been in denial and then so crushed when she did die? The what ifs are the things that linger and torment even now, almost thirty years later.

In the period between my mom's death and my dad's death, I would, as is common with PTSD, replay over and over in my head the events surrounding my mother's death. This was mostly on holidays, her birthday, and the anniversary of her death. But after my dad died, I would retell the story of my mom's passing, over and over in my head as a narrative in great detail, every day all day, any time I wasn't preoccupied thinking about something else. I guess that this is the "post" in PTSD. The medical professionals tell you to let go of the regret and guilt, but for me that hasn't been possible. I have learned to forgive myself some, and to remind myself that my mom knew that I loved her and that she would want me to move on. That does help somewhat, but there will always be some part of me that won't ever be able to get past it. Oddly, writing this book has helped. And I hope that reading it will help others, at least a little.

With regards to the agoraphobia, as with any mental illness there is a wide range and degree to which people suffer. What is agoraphobia to me is most likely not the same as it would be to someone else. So when I say, "agoraphobia," I am speaking only about my own experiences. As I have stated elsewhere in this book, my problems started with a panic attack in a very crowded bowling ally. I had always been self-conscious in public situations. I was usually the biggest kid in the crowd. I always stood out in the room, or at least I thought I did. I have pretty much been noticeably taller and bigger than the average guy. In my last year of junior high school, I hit six feet and two hundred pounds. I am currently 6' 4" and weigh about 260 pounds. I have never been an extroverted person. In fact, I am just the opposite, and I have always gone out of my way to avoid social situations.

So since that first panic attack, I have been terrified of going through that ever again. I avoided going out for the first few weeks after my panic attack, and it became almost impossible to leave the house. Today, if I go out, my wife goes with me, and I will also take a Xanax, depending on the situation. As I have said, it can be tough to just go get the mail, or to the corner to get my daughter off the school bus. I try to time it so that the bus has already dropped the kids off and pulled away, and the other parents have started to walk to their houses. I can just walk about halfway down the street and have my daughter come to me.

When I do go out, within about a half a mile from home, I get anxious and feel like it is hard to breathe. Then I'll get lightheaded, and if I haven't taken my Xanax, the anxiety just keeps building. On more than one occasion, we have had to turn around so I could take some meds or just stay home. The same holds true if someone is coming over to our house, depending on who it is and what the reason for the visit is. The worst situations are places I don't have control over. If I think that my leaving the place would draw attention to me, then I just won't go. For example, if I had just ordered food in a restaurant and started to have a panic attack, it would be awkward, to say the least, to leave before the food even came. Or on a trip to the barber, what if I freaked out before my haircut was done? I couldn't just get up and leave. Those are just a few examples of the kind of situations that I avoid putting myself into. So if it comes up that there is some place that we want or need to go, I have to think through all the angles before I even commit to going.

Chapter 15
Mind Control

There used to be a public-service announcement on television years ago that said, "A mind is a terrible thing to waste." During the last five or six years, I have sometimes thought that "A mind is a terrible thing—period." I will never cease to be totally amazed by the ways your brain can really mess with you. It can really take over.

At times, I was convinced that if I didn't do something on my schedule at the exact time, I was just asking for trouble. Now the "normal" me knew that nothing bad, good, or otherwise was going to happen, yet dammed if I didn't freak out and do this "something" just in case. If I had a dollar for every time I was convinced that I was having a heart attack or stroke or some other really bad medical problem, I would be a rich man. And each time some small part of me would know that in reality there was nothing physically wrong with me, but a bigger part of me was sure I should rush to the nearest emergency room. Actually a large part of the problem is really my brain sending my body the fight-or-flight signal, and my body reacting in many very physical ways. These include sweating, feeling lightheaded, and feeling my heart pounding, to name a few. When that happens, it is very hard if not impossible, to believe that you aren't having some medical problem.

Likewise, a simple thing like a little sunshine or a few clouds can have me soaring or crashing mentally. I have learned that negative thoughts are about a hundred times stronger than normal or happy thoughts. And I am sure that it's very hard to be around someone whose mood can change from hour to hour, if not minute to minute. A lot of the time I can feel that my mood is changing, and I have no clue why it's happening.

Another thing that has become common is that I can have whole days or weeks where I feel as though I have really turned a corner, only to slip back into being sure that I will never get back to "normal." Mental illness can be a wild roller coaster ride. And your ticket can be out of your control.

Chapter 16
The Internet—
Helping or Hurting?

I think that one of the ways that I might be luckier than agoraphobics of many years ago is that I have access to all of the technology that is available today. I can't imagine being home, day after day, with no internet and only four or five channels on the TV. Cable TV, with its one hundred to two hundred channels, offers a lot of distraction, 24/7. And with the internet, the number of hours you can spend online is incredible. And I have never been in a chat room or tried to blog. But even without doing those things, the internet offers so much to anyone who is or has to be home all day and night. I kept in touch with family and friends through email. I kept up on the news of the world online. And I did research about my problems (i.e. anxiety and mental-illness issues). There are many very good websites available.

At the same time, I guess you could make an argument that the internet also has a downside, in that it allows you to have a false sense of connection with the world at large. When you can check the news, shop, search for sites of interest, and communicate with family and friends online, you can make yourself believe that you have put in a fairly normal day, without ever leaving the house.

Also, it gives you a place to waste an awful lot of time, and that has many ups and downs. In the end, I would say the internet has more upside than downside, and I am glad that I have had it available to me all these years.

A simple Google search will net hundreds or thousands of sites that will allow you to reach out to others. It will allow you to find out how common your condition is. It can also help you form a diagnosis of sorts on just what is wrong with you. But I would caution against doing too much self diagnosing, leave that up to the professionals. The information you gather from the internet can help you discuss your situation with a doctor, and can even help you find a doctor who treats your specific problems. I just searched the internet, scanning several sites , I saw that the number of Americans with some type and degree of mental health illness is in the millions. One site put it at over eight million, another said that it is on the rise.

Chapter 17
Disconnected

It's funny that, having talked about the internet as a way of making connections with family, friends, and the outside world in general, my next topic is the feeling of being so disconnected with all those same things. I have felt a disconnection in every sense of the word on many, many occasions.

There have been many times when I have been at home with my wife and children and felt completely alone, as if I were invisible or seeing everything from outside. It is a very distant feeling. Also, I would feel this when my family went out, whether to visit other family or friends, go to a school function, or go out for a day of normal recreation. Staying home alone on those occasions felt worse than just being lonely. There were thoughts of guilt that my family, especially my children, might feel like I just didn't want to spend time with them, or that I didn't care about their concerts or school plays or baseball games or whatever it was that I was missing.

Plus, there is a great deal of regret that I missed out on so much of my family's lives outside of home. Those hours and days would just drag on and on. And the more times I didn't go out, the harder it was to leave when I really had to go out. I would put so much pressure on the simplest outing. After missing a few social events, it made it impossible to go because now I would have to face others, knowing that they knew I missed previous visits because of anxiety. It just kind of snowballs. The more I'd miss, the harder it would be to go out.

Chapter 18
Journaling

One of the tools that was suggested to me by my psychologist, Lisa to help with different types of psychological illness is journaling. I will admit that I probably did not give it a good enough effort, nor try hard enough to learn how to do it right, but it just didn't seem to work for me. Below are the extent of the entries for a journal I kept for just a few months. In spite of my poor results, I would recommend journaling to others, but I suggest that you seek guidance to get the best results.

05/08/06
"Yesterday was a rough day. I had a nasty anxiety attack. VERY anxious the first half of the day. The last week or so my mood has really nosed dived. I think it has to do with the weather getting nicer. I think it signals the start of another change of seasons, and that means another year is speeding past. Also, when the weather is this nice it really sucks being 'trapped' inside. In the winter it is easy to stay inside, and not feel to bad about it. Well, it's going to be a LONG summer."

05/15/06

"Rainy, blah Monday. Monday's suck, it's back to my routine and the day alone with no way to go somewhere. Maybe just a drive or to the park or the lake. There is no good place to go, to just sit and chill within walking distance."05/17/06

"BORED !!! Tired!!!!!

It sucks that all entries so far have been so negative. Feel like a whiner. How do I get out of this mess? A good three or four years have gone by and I've done nothing! I could have done so much with this 'free time.' Built something, written something etc. But I have nothing to show for this time. Well I'm going to leave it here, writing this is just making me feel like crap!"

05/22/06

"Today Charisse was off work. We were going to go out, do a little shopping or just drive around or whatever. But I have a cold or flu and don't feel well. When Charisse is off the days go by so fast!

I really feel much better mentally whenever Charisse and I go out. Even if we just go to the store or whatever. I know Charisse enjoys it to, she tells me so, each time we go out. Crazy that that's our big thrill, but it really is, we have always enjoyed spending time together. I never really looked at it from Charisse's point of view, but I guess leaving without your spouse 99.9% of the time you go out, must stink, so I guess she's just happy with whatever she gets. I am very lucky that she can understand what I am going through. She's great!"

05/27/06

"Beginning of the Memorial Day weekend. Didn't do much today, it went by too fast, hope the rest of the weekend goes by a little slower. Going to try to go to the cemetery tomorrow. I have always gone to the cemetery on holidays but I have missed a few times this year. Didn't go on Mother's Day, which was the first Mother's Day I have missed since Mom died in 1979.

I have been going to a new psychologist since just after Easter, talking about my problems with her is reopening all those old wounds, so I think that's why I didn't make it to the cemetery this Mother's Day. I know I'll never get over my Mom's death, but I am working on all the extra baggage from it. I have to be hopeful, and give it a good try."

05/30/06

"Almost time to go get Anna off the school bus. Not looking forward to it, it's eight-eight degrees or hotter and very humid. I'll be a sweating, dripping mess by the time we get back. I hate hot weather.

05/31/06

"WOW!! Totally bored!! It's very hot out again today (nineties). I have been trying to start walking each day but not in this weather.

I was online a few minutes ago, and even that was boring. It's like my brain has shut down. I am drawing a blank every time I try to think about something to do. What a waste of time.

Tired, very tired."

06/07/06

"Well I am a total wreck about going to Gene and Mary's house (Charisse's dad and his wife). I really want to see Sue (Charisse's sister who is in town from Fla.). But I haven't been over to Gene's house in at least a year. So my being there is going to draw some attention. It's just kind of overwhelming. And I feel like such a wimp saying or writing that I am so overwhelmed. Oh well we'll see what happens tonight. I really don't know if I will go or not."

06/07/06

"Wow, I went and I am very glad I did!!!"

06/16/06

"What a day, a total piece of crap!! I had an appointment with a new psychiatrist, I stopped going to the last one because she always made me wait for forty-five min. or more. And all I needed was for her to do is renew my prescriptions. So Lisa (my psychologist) recommended this doctor.

Anyway I was stressed out all morning, we even had to turn around on the way to his office so I could take a Xanax.

And boy what an asshole he was. In a nutshell it was his way or the highway. No compassion at all. Arrogant S.O.B. Needless to say I won't be going back to him. But now I have to worry who will write my prescriptions. Lisa is great but she can't prescribe meds. I have about thirty days worth so I have two weeks to get an order in for my meds, since we do mail-order prescriptions. If it were up to me I would just stop taking them all together, I hate being on them. But Charisse freaked out when

I mentioned not taking them to her. I am sure she's right, I am just tired of messing with doctors."

06/19/06

"In a funk!! Don't know what else to say, I am just in a major funk. Learned over the weekend that my best friend's mother passed away over the weekend. I was already in this funk from late last week, just can't shake it. I am so freaking sick of my life. Same old thing every day. And I am clueless as to how to pull myself out of my funk. It's weird how you can feel so all alone, even when you're not. Thank God for Charisse, she's the only thing keeping me going. Can hardly remember what it feels like to be 'normal.' I have lost so many years of my life to this 'problem' and sadly I don't know if I have reached bottom or if there is worse to come?"

06/22/06

"Wow, what a day. Took a Xanax and went to my friend Pete's mother's funeral. There aren't many things I can go out for, but I was not going to miss this. I have known Pete and his family for over thirty years. I didn't go to the wake last night, unbelievably it was at the same funeral home that both my parents were at, and there was no way I could go.

Anyway it was good to see the Doncevics , they are without question the nicest family I know, each one of them is just as friendly as possible. They are good people. So it was very important for me to go today. And I am proud and happy I went. "

0?/0?/06

"It has been a little while since my last entry. And I don't think I will be doing any more entries. I have been awfully negative with this journal and don't think that's very helpful to my healing. Also I think if I am going to write anything I should be working on my Book.

It has seemed over the last few years that my book would never get written, but I owe it to myself to give it a real try. I guess in the end the question is if I do write it will anyone want it?"

Chapter 19
Man's Best Friend

Over the course of my illness, I have seen at least one report on television about the use of dogs to help people with certain mental and emotional problems. I have had a few dogs in my life and have always been very fond of all dogs. We, mostly my daughter and I, have wanted a dog for quite some time, but my oldest son is very allergic to them. So we put it off until two years ago when my son was planning to move out. We checked out different types of dogs until we came across the doodle family of dogs (i.e. labradoodle and goldendoodle). We found a labradoodle that was within our budget and bought it.

She is a female named Angel. And since I was home 24/7, she and I became very close very quickly. After we'd had her for just three or four months I went into the hospital for emergency surgery. I was in for eight days, and she actually became physically ill after the first few days I was gone. While I was still in the hospital, my wife took Angel to the vet, who asked if there was anything going on at home. My wife told her about my being hospitalized. The vet said that was indeed the problem. Angel has been a huge help to me, getting me out of the house for walks and out to play in the yard. Also, the time I spend with her is time I am not just sitting around thinking about my situation, and that is a big help. Now I know a dog is not for everybody, but I can say having Angel has been helpful and calming, In fact, there have been times when I have had a panic attack at home, and she has come over to lay next to me. I found that as I was petting her, and didn't even know it, my panic attack would lessen some. God bless our pets.

Chapter 20
Superhuman Strength

There have been times over the years, that in spite of the agoraphobia, the anxiety, and the panic attacks, I found the strength to do things that I wouldn't have believed possible. The commonality among them is family. An example of this is attending my son's graduation commencement. More common are the times when a member of my immediate family faced some medical emergency.

On, I believe, three occasions, we had to take my daughter to the emergency room for asthma. Each time she was admitted, I would be the one who would stay overnight with her for the two or three days and nights that she was hospitalized. And most recently, just over a month ago, my wife had a medical emergency. On the Saturday of Thanksgiving weekend, she took our dog out for a walk early in the morning. Near the end of the walk, she felt her heart racing and was lightheaded. After trying for a few hours to see if it would subside, she said she wanted to go to the hospital. I went upstairs to change, and when I came back down after just a few minutes, she was laying on the couch and telling me to call 911. Over the next few hours things got pretty tense, first waiting for the ambulance, then taking the ride to the hospital, and then waiting for a diagnoses. Of those three things, the ride to the hospital was by far the worst. My poor daughter sat up front with the driver, and I was in the back with my wife and two paramedics, who were having a hard time getting her heart rate to slow down. They were in contact with the hospital, and it seemed like even the paramedics were a little anxious. She ended up being hospitalized for four days and having to have a procedure call a heart ablation. I had to rely on my Xanax pretty heavily over those four days. My point is that there are times when even a severe agoraphobic can have stretches of "normalcy," albeit with the help of medication.

Chapter 21
Final Thoughts

I would like to conclude this book with a story about how I was able to overcome my illness and go on to live a "normal" life. I would also like to conclude this book with the answers to all the questions that you might have about how you too can beat your illness and go on to live a "normal" life.

I would like to do this. But this is real life, and I have not found nor do I believe I will find the answers to all my questions, or those that many of you have.

As I sit here today, I still have agoraphobia and all the rest of the alphabet soup of mental and emotional problems. I am still on medication and still seeing a counselor. However, I do feel as though I have made progress. I also have learned that progress can be fleeting. I can say that recently I have been doing some activities that I probably couldn't have done not too long ago. Also, I think I am starting to get it. After years of banging my head into a wall, I do believe that I understand the process I need to stick to, and that it will help me get my life back. After years of trial and error, it has sunk in that there will be steps forward and some steps backward. But I can't let a backward step allow me to fall two or three steps farther. Instead, I need to (and think I can) hold my ground and maintain that single backward step, pause, get my head straight. and take two or three steps forward.

If I can pass two things on to you. it's the importance of patience and self-forgiveness. Patience is important because, although it sounds so simplistic, it took a while for you to get to the point you're at. So why would you think you could get back to where you were any quicker? If anything, it may well take longer because you have some new mountains to climb that weren't around. When you slip, and slip farther than you ever thought possible, it shakes you to your core and can shatter your self-confidence. So you first have to learn to trust and have faith in yourself before you can really start to heal.

Self forgiveness is important because, as I have learned, there is a very strong instinct to be harder on yourself than others are on you. But you must accept the failures as easily as the triumphs. Beating yourself up over a slip here and another slip there will not only hold you back, but will also make you fall farther back in your recovery.

In closing, I would like to thank you, because the process of writing this book has really been helpful in my own recovery. And I hope that some or all of this book will be useful in helping you find your way through the ups and downs of your own struggle, as you work toward getting your life back and finding a place where you are comfortable with who you are and how you live. Always remember that you are not alone. There are many other people out there who share your struggle, and there are many people who would like to and can help you find your way. All along, my biggest mistake has been to feel like I could do this alone, and that I didn't want other people to even know about my situation. And yet here I am today, writing a book for the whole world to see, and I think it may well be one of the best things I have done yet to begin real healing. May we all find our way back to who we once were and want to be again.

Chapter 22
Update

Well, here it is about a year since I finished my manuscript. By now it was supposed to be a published book flying off the shelves. OK, maybe not flying off the shelves, but I did really think it would be published. I learned very quickly after I sent out my first few proposals that it wasn't going to be quite that easy. I sent out well over a hundred e-mail proposals and received only about a dozen replies. All but one of those was the standard "Thanks and good luck, but we're not interested." One person said that she might be interested, but she was very busy so I should get back to her in three or four months. So I waited and then sent her a complete manuscript, and I waited and waited some more. I e-mailed her a reminder, and she said that she was sorry but hadn't gotten to it. She said she would get back to me in a week or two. Well that never happened, so my manuscript just sat in a drawer until a few weeks ago, when I decided that I would publish it myself.

I am doing an update because, after many anxious months (maybe even a year or more), I decided to take the advice of my wife and my counselor Lisa, who have been trying to get me to try new meds. I knew that the combination of meds I was taking was not really working, but as I have said many times in this book, I hate switching meds. There are often side effects when getting off the old meds and then more side effects getting on the new, and I had had some bad experiences with changing prescriptions in the past. Another thing that held me back was that I got my prescriptions from my family doctor, and it was nice that he didn't make me see him when a prescription ran out. I know that this setup wasn't really good for me in the long run, but it was nice not to have to go in every few months and see the doctor to get my prescription renewed. Anyway, I knew that I would have to go to a new psychiatrist to get on new medication, and I had not had good luck in the past with psychiatrists. But my counselor Lisa, who was not licensed to prescribe medication, assured me that she had just the right doctor for me.

I put off for some time going to see the new doctor. But 2009 was a very bad year for me, and by January of 2010, I was more depressed than I had ever been. And I was just scared enough about how I was feeling that I had nowhere else to turn.

It started in 2007, when at the age of forty-eight, I had to go in to the hospital for emergency gallbladder surgery. That might not sound like that big a deal to most people, but for someone with anxiety, OCD, panic attacks, PTSD, and all the stuff that comes with those, I was freaking out. I have always been scared to death about any type of surgery, and I was so thankful that for the first forty-eight years of my life I had never had a broken bone, a stitch, or even a night in a hospital. It turned out that I had been in denial about some pains I had been having on and off for over a year, and it got much more serious than I ever imagined. When the surgeon talked to my wife, he told her that I had the worst gallbladder he had ever seen. I spent eight days in the hospital. A week later, when I went to his office to have the staples removed, he got the pathology report back. He said I was very lucky that I didn't wait any longer because my gallbladder had become gangrenous, and had it leaked or spread it could have killed me. So now I freak every time I have any kind of pain. Anyway, it took a few months to recover from the surgery, but things got back to normal.

The year 2009 didn't start out very well and only got worse as the year went by. In January I had pretty nasty shoulder pain in the morning or if I leaned to my left against the arm of a chair or couch. So I went to see my doctor, who prescribed an anti-inflammatory, thinking I most likely had arthritis. But a few weeks later the pain just got more frequent and much more painful. It got to the point where I ended up going to the ER in some of the worst pain I have ever felt. The doctor in the ER give me some pain meds and muscle relaxants, and he referred me to a specialist. A few days later I saw the specialist. He gave me more meds and a prescription for an MRI. He said for me to take the meds for two weeks, and if I was still in pain to go for the MRI. Well, I lasted only one week, and the pain just got worse in spite of the heavy-duty pain meds I was on. I had the MRI, and the very next day the specialist called and asked me to come in that day. When we got there, he told me I would definitely need to have Anterior Cervical Spinal Fusion surgery to repair a ruptured disc . He sent me to a surgeon who turned out to be one of the best in Cleveland. He had already gotten a copy of my MRI from the other doctor, and he and got right to the point. I saw him on a Thursday, and he said he could do the operation the following Tuesday or I would have to wait for over two weeks because he was going on vacation. So my anxiety level was now in overdrive, and I had to make a decision pretty much on the spot. But the pain overrode the anxiety, and I said I would have it done the following Tuesday. Looking back, it really is a good thing that the pain was so bad, and that I had been suffering for at least three weeks by then, or I am sure I would have chickened out and put off the surgery for as long as I could. But between the pain, and the lesson I learned from ignoring the symptoms of my gallbladder problem, I knew I had no choice.

As I have said earlier and often in this book, it's been my experience that when you are agoraphobic for a few years or more, leaving the house only one or two times a month (and then mostly for doctors' appointments), you feel as though you have wasted those years of your life, and that really takes a toll on you mentally. So here I was about to turn fifty, a time when some people have that midlife crisis, and that's where I was, big time. I had never had any really serious physical health problems, and now I had two pretty serious surgeries in a two-year period.

The neck surgery consisted of making an incision in the front of my throat, then moving everything out of the way so they could reach my spine. The surgeons removed the bad discs and put in a little piece of cadaver bone in its place. They used a metal plate and two screws to hold it all in place. I went home the next afternoon with a large neck brace that I had to wear for six to seven weeks, 24/7. I could not move my head at all. I spent most of the next six weeks sitting in a recliner.

At this point the last thing I needed was to be stuck in a chair most of the day with little to do. My grandmother's saying was "An idle mind is the devil's playground." I would change that to "The idle mind of an agoraphobic with severe anxiety is worse than the devil's playground." I had so much time, much of it alone, to beat myself up over wasting years of my life and not having any idea when or how my life would change, if at all.

So to recap, I was now fifty years old, felt I had wasted the last three or four years of my life, and had no hope that anything would change for the better any time soon. Plus, it seemed like my body was falling apart.

When I got the brace off, the doctor sent me for five or six weeks of physical therapy. My first appointment went pretty well. My wife and I were in a room with a therapist, who evaluated me and explained what I would be doing. I told her about my anxiety, but neither one of us thought that would be a problem. I thought that it would be my wife, the therapist, and me in a room each time. I was scheduled to go two or three times a week. So I went for my second appointment, and it was a different therapist, who said my wife could wait in the lobby while I got my therapy. OK that kind of threw me a curve ball. Then she took me to a large room with other patients. The therapist had me start working out, but now my anxiety was way over the top. To make matters worse, it seemed like everybody knew everybody, and some of them asked me questions. Even the Xanax I had taken before I left home wasn't enough to help me. I pretty much tried not to make eye contact with anyone and acted like I was really into my exercises and couldn't be bothered. That got me through the session. When we got in the car to go home, my wife already knew there was no way I was going back again. When I got home, I emailed the physical therapist and explained that

I just couldn't come back because of my anxiety. She emailed back and wished me luck on my neck recovery. It wasn't more than a few days before I realized that I had an appointment with the surgeon, and he would want to know how my therapy was going. On the day of my appointment with the surgeon I literally ran away from home!

My wife was home, ready to drive me to the doctor, and I said, "Go ahead out to the car and get the air conditioner on, and I will be right out." As soon as she went out to the garage, I went out the front door and took off on foot. I was so embarrassed that I couldn't go to the doctor that I couldn't even face my wife and tell her I, so I ran away. I walked to a park and sat on a bench for several hours before heading home. On the way home, I ran into my wife, who had been out looking for me and was worried sick about where I went and why. I'm sure she was also mad, but she didn't show it (she's the greatest). So I called the doctor to reschedule, and as it turned out, it was weeks before I would get in to see him as he had lost his father and took some time off. So when I did see him the next time, he never even mentioned the physical therapy.

So now it was the end of summer 2009, and I was feeling as depressed as I ever had. But it would get worse. September 6 is the anniversary of my mom's passing, and this year marked thirty years since she had died. I know people say that time heals all wounds, but for me it just made me sadder, because it meant it had now been thirty years since I had seen my mother. It had been thirty years since I had talked to her, thirty years since everything with my mom. In the beginning, when you lose someone you often think to yourself, "Oh, it was just last week that we talked about this or that, just a couple of weeks since we had done this or done that." But now it was thirty years! I remember in the weeks after she passed, I would pick up something around the house and think, "Mom held this or used that." Some things still had the scent of her perfume. But now there is nothing. So I was getting more depressed than I ever thought possible.

I believe that there is something after our life on earth, and that we will see loved ones who have passed. At times during this period, I thought, "OK, I am ready to go. I miss her too much and would be OK dying if it meant I would get to see her." Between thoughts like that and the holidays, mostly Christmas, the year ended with me in a very bad place, so much that it scared me, because I had never been this depressed. I worried about what would it be like if it got worse. So by January 2010 I knew I had to see a new psychiatrist and get put on new medications.

So that brings me back to where I started this chapter. Sorry for taking the long way here, but I really felt that I needed to give some context for why I finally agreed to see a new psychiatrist. I know things are getting bad when I do things like make doctors' appointments myself instead of having my wife do it. I was ready, so I called and set up the appointment. And when that day came, I was nervous but ready, sort of like with my surgeries. You put it off and put it off, and then all of a sudden it's almost like you say, "How could I have put this off for so long?"

After talking to the doctor, he said that he wanted to take me off of the Xanax and have me try something new. I wasn't sure, and told him so. I told him that I had grown pretty attached to the Xanax, and I really couldn't see going without it. This was sort of funny, because I was only taking it for three things. One was each night to help me sleep. The other times were when I was going out or people were coming over, and I also took it when I would start to have a panic attack. But I was having panic attacks more often, many times at home and for no apparent reason. But I always had my Xanax with me—always! So the idea of giving it up was hard to take. But the doctor was pretty cool. He knew where I was coming from, and he said he'd write me a prescription for the new medication, Klonopin. When I felt ready, I could get it filled and start taking it. That was huge. The idea that he would let me get comfortable and change the medications on my own was really helpful and made the switch much easier. After a few days, I got the prescription filled, and after a few more days I switched. I stopped using my beloved Xanax and started Klonopin. The medication is used, among other things, for anxiety. The doctor thought that if we could control the anxiety, it would help a lot with the depression. In addition to adding the Klonopin, he increased my Zoloft but left my Wellbutrin where it was. Within just a few weeks, my panic attacks at home, the ones that came on for what seemed like no reason at all, pretty much went away. The doctor has had me go out more on my own, since I've been on the Klonopin for a while. When I've gone out, it hasn't always gone well, but at least it doesn't stop me from trying again a few days or weeks later. I have noticed that the Klonopin seems to be a little less effective lately. It could just be my imagination. When I see my doctor in a few weeks, maybe we'll increase the dosage?

So if there is anything I would like people to get from this update, it's that I know it sucks to switch medications that you are used to and comfortable with. Often you run into some side effects getting on or off most of the medications for mental illness. It really is worth the try. And it definitely is better than staying on something that isn't working for you. I have done that in the past out of fear of the unknown.

I still have bouts of depression, but it is the kind I can and have dealt with before, not the very scary and hopeless kind I was having. I wish you all get the right doctor and the right medications at the right time for you. And if we can't eliminate these illnesses that are stealing our lives, let's pray we can control them.

God bless you and good luck!

I will be setting up a website, *www.usedto-benormal.com* , where I hope others like me will exchange stories and information that might help one another. My email address is *usedtobenormal@gmail.com* .

I look forward to hearing from anyone who would like to share his or her stories. I would love to hear from young veterans or have a space on my site where they can talk to one another , to share their stories and lean on each other when needed. If you know any of these troops who have had to serve two, three, four or more tours overseas, reach out to them. Give to charities that help them deal with their mental health issues. They served us and we need to be there for them. God Bless them and their families.